Other books by André Swartley:

THE ISLAND OF MISFIT TOYS
2006 Indiana Book Award Finalist

AMERICANUS REX
2010 Next Generation Indie Book Awards Fiction Finalist

LEON MARTIN AND THE FANTASY GIRL
2013 Dante Rossetti Awards Finalist

THE WRETCHED AFTERLIFE OF ODETTA KOOP

Published by Workplay Publishing
Newton, KS 67114

workplaypublishing.com

Copyright © 2025 André Swartley
All rights reserved.

ISBN 978-1-7343946-6-5

Cover photo & design, interior layout, and illustrations by André Swartley

Characters, locations and events in this novel are products of the author's imagination or are used fictitiously. Resemblance to actual places, historical events or people, living or dead, is purely coincidental.

PRINTED IN THE UNITED STATES OF AMERICA

THE BALLAD OF
MOON BOG

haunted poems & plays

written & illustrated by

André Swartley

Workplay Publishing

For O & S

POEMS

O! the comfort

of many ghosts

versus the terror

of just one

Prelude

I was up briefly in the night, with dreams
Clawing upward through funnel webs inverted
Gossamer cones still as yesterday's breeze
Threads clinging to fingertips
Even as shapes collapse and drift to darkness
Unseen spinners weave unlived horrors
Fantasy full and sweet
Groaning with the daily venom of the mind

The Ballad of Moon Bog

The light is never quite right in Moon Bog
Lavender and yellow and green as a bruise
A greasy sheen lays on the water day and night
Irridescent, noxious, lovely
Locals wrongly blame the old mine

A riot of life thrives in Moon Bog
To the consternation of many in town
In earthy patches where cold water has not
Yet crept, underbrush sways and rustles
Claws coax waves from thick fronds

An owl dives like a seabird into dry green waves
Surfaces wide-eyed and wider-mouthed
Pink feet and a fuzzy round bottom bulge
From her gullet, gold-ringed eyes survey
Silent feathers bush out and resettle, satisfied

Fleshy mushrooms capped in yellow—more gold
rings of Moon Bog—luxuriate among mossy trunks
Ripe as any fruit, each a savory feast fried in butter
As long as one can divine them from their pale
Orange deadly brethren, of course

At sundown every hue of Moon Bog swells like
The bullfrogs bellowing the day's requiem
Crickets saw out a maddening harmony
Only the greasy water stills, as if to better mirror
The torrential shafts of color through the trees

In one dark, cozy corner new light flares
A gas lamp creaks on a hook, echoing the crickets
A cat yowls for scritches in that good spot
Behind his ear, and a woman's voice, thick
As honeyed wine, hums the tune of the night

Water & Smoke

The spirits barter for water and smoke
    Vapors feeding on vapors

Some rive the ground in the back garden
    Part earth with lazy strokes

Some visit the upstairs hallway
    Peer through doorways, creak floorboards

Still others cocoon themselves in trees
    Perturb leaves with wakeful, twilit stretches

They come when called, mostly
    Arrive hungry and thirsty

Those who recall may crave
    Whiskey, vodka, craft beer, Dr. Pepper

A bowl of cherries, a crunchy granola bar
    Pressed like plywood in glazed twin planks

But it is water that nourishes all comers
    A mug on the sill, a Ball jar on the countertop

Then, a libation of fragrant smoke
    The charred head of a penny match

Those with jaws unhinge them wide
    Open caverns in their throats

Gorge the smoke down bulging python necks
    Become the smoke, fractal and keen

Though yet, again, the water
    An ounce on the endtable, a brimmed thimble

A feast for strangers, a communal treasure
    So simple a thing, shared

Calls, drives, sates, and binds
    A phantom maelstrom, eager on the doorstep

Lucy

Another daughter has vanished from Whitton
Her name was Lucy but everyone called her ****

She was fifteen and still is, assuming time
Behaves the same outside Whitton as within

Lucy loved boys and flowers, people laughed
She kept a box turtle, Roars, who too is now gone

Whispers hissed gravely and with appropriate
Sympathy over clean placemats seem to suggest

Lucy's (though they say ****'s) turtle may have
gone first, flushed down a toilet, they surmise

By her terrible older brother, God love him, who
struggled with his temper, like their father

God love him, who's had a hard go since the mine
Closed, and that's why Lucy (though they say ****)

Disappeared, ran away, perhaps, from a hard home
Not that she made things easy for herself…

"Or her family!" they hasten to whisper
Noddingly across long, straight fencetops

What with her sundresses and long hair and
The way she drew flowers in her notebook

"Just knock it off, ****!" they bawled at school,
In the town park, at the ice cream stand, and at

Church, where she ought to have shown more
Respect. "Don't you know how hard your dad

And brother already have it?" they demanded
With appropriate gravity and sympathy

Then—*POOF!*—she was gone from Whitton
With or possibly without Roars the box turtle

Some say she ran away, but they always say that
And frankly it's getting hard to believe now

Others blame the witch, of course, but The Watch
Say her house is too small to hold all these kids

Whitton is home to more monsters
Than she, and little Ricken Scaggs, that's right

Ricken the pastor's middle son, swears he found a
Fingernail lying in the road near a manhole cover

A sure sign that The Snatcher took another victim
Little Ricken, too young yet to join The Watch

Talks often of The Snatcher, about its long
Hooked nose and throbbing tentacle hair and

Even though no one else has seen this beast
They've begun to whisper, gravely, sympathetically

What if little Ricken actually saw something?
Where else, after all, would all these children go?

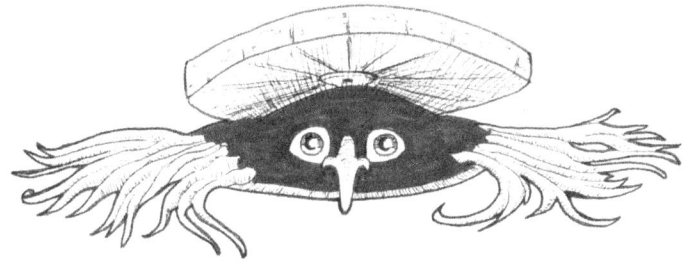

The Watch

Legends about her abound
    that haughty temptress whose
    glowing cabin on Moon Bog
    hosts the ruin of men's virtue

Any one tale of her doings would turn
    a man's hair shock-white in a streak
    down the center of his scalp like
    the stripe of a skunk, nature's pariah

She launders her woolens in the nude, you know
    when she thinks she's alone, unaware
    pious watchers leer through bramble
    sunk to the knees in glutinous muck

Men in town call it "The Watch"
    they skulk in pairs to the greenest patch
    of the forest where only the Devil
    could inspire such raucous, vibrant life

And, oh, the Devil is cruelly fair, acts as
      though she cannot see them Watch her
      preen, pose, squeeze red berry
      juice to full lips, admiring in the water

For whom? the Watch hiss to one another
      true, it has been long since one was taken
      but each day brings the next temptation
      another hapless man doomed to pleasure

Their poor wives, these brave men who squat
      in cold slime, rapt for tease or jiggle
      that will mean their time has come
      at last a little death to presage damnation

The Witch

Standing deadly still
Her hair streams out behind her
No breeze stirs the leaves

Imperiled Souls

The men return tired and damp
The women pause and soothe

The men who, after all, shield the town's souls
The women, in contrast, merely maintain

The men's families, homes, schedules, and
The women's—i.e. their own—business that

The men peer loftily above, fixed on the souls of
The women: the eyes, ears, heart, lungs, bones of

The men's own survival; yet how compares that to
The women's imperiled souls

The Snake

You've been right all along
It's slithering toward you
Hissing its song

It will turn all the children
Corrupt all the youth
Draw black-eyed brethren

The snake to its prize
In the blink of a blink
In the breath between sighs

Your worst fear now true
Others—all the others
Did it better than you

The House on Star Mount

He lied in every word, and he owned every thing
His house, one of them, stood above others
On a hill longtimers called Star Mount
An exaggeration but a fond one, since everyone,
Excluding the Liar, had made memories there

The Liar, who liked nothing of his own,
Liked the hill because they liked it

He made grand noises when buying the hill
To let it endure for generations
Then, the thing bought, promptly, obviously,
razed the summit flat for his new art deco house
That would rear high above all others in town

And, not coincidentally, blot out the eastern sky
For everyone in town save himself

Post-razing came a raising: a high metal fence
Around the base of the hill—sorry, *plateau*—
With a motorized gate for heavy construction
Vehicles that left the macadam pitted and rough
The Liar drove over a pothole and dented a rim

Presently an editorial ran in the town paper
Decrying neglect of the town's infrastructure

The next week a local fence maker wrote as well
Pointing out how the Liar's extravagant
Private construction was to blame for the pits
The Liar bought the newspaper promising
To bring a balanced perspective to local media

In practice this meant shuttering the print shop,
Moving online, and advertising payday loans

On the forest side of Star Mount, the Liar clearcut
Old growth trees and laid a sprawling garden
Of exotic ornamental flowers that withered
And rotted in the sodden soil, giving off
A sweet, yeasty stink like a donut shop dumpster

Only the green bamboo grove thrived, reached,
stabbed out hungrily, miles into the wetland

The Sign

All noted the sign as they drove past
White script on maroon background

Perfect simplicity awash in headlights
Flowing font, the single word *Felgers*

All paid the sign its due, each meditating
on its significance, a similar thought

Universally shared but voiced by only one:
"Is there anything it can't do?"

As all had mind-spake the same, down to
The word, none needed answer or dispute

Night Terror

An hour after sleep
Hard, dry sponge grates live synapse
Bass drum steps approach

The Long Tooth

We are wired to dream of teeth
    But not the good kind

In dreams teeth go missing, split
    Crack into rubble

Crumbling concrete pillars, condemned
    Nerve clusters snarl like old rebar

The one that comes to me, though
    When I recall not sleeping:

A dream of a central incisor, long
    jagged as a cartoon bolt of lightning

The bottom edge rasps my lapel
    Dimples fabric when I glance downward

How have I come so far, I wonder
    Without snapping it right off?

No matter, it is my Now, to be cradled
    Babied to the detriment of all else, forever

Because although I have just noticed it
    In the dream I cannot imagine another life

The Manston

Really "infestation" is too strong a word. They're brown recluse, more or less the size of a quarter with a little guitar shape on their back like they're always in the mood for dinner and a song.

One scuttled up out of the drain on the side of the kitchen sink I never use and put up her dukes like she wanted to fight me for flooding her front door. They're actually fine though.

What you have to do is, you grasp your t-shirt by the hem across the shoulders and whip the whole thing up and down in case one crept in there while the shirt was rumpled on the floor last night.

This morning I reached for a sock laying at the foot of the bed and saw the toe kind of hopping and bopping. No big deal. Did the same trick as with the t-shirt and the little guy came rocketing out.

He rolled a couple times on the floor before wobbling away to squeeze under a crack between the oak moulding and the floor. He's still there; one little crook of his leg is still sticking out.

It's not like it's a chore to bang your shoes upside down on the floor a few times before you go out.

People are only afraid because—well okay they can be dangerous if you don't stay aware of potential hiding spots. Or if you don't check for bites. The bites don't show up right away, see.

Just two little baby needles snapping down quick as a flash. Barely break the skin. And not every bite leads to necrosis and skin grafts and all that.
I mean, that one on the back of my leg did.

I won't show you but I've got a crater of a scar back there like someone took a red hot ice cream scoop to my hamstring. But I'd left those sweatpants on the bathroom floor for like two days, so.

My sister won't bring my niece over anymore. I mean, what is her problem, right? She grew up here same as me but suddenly the spiders are too much? She moved out and got all sensitive.

No, it's true the venom can be more dangerous for kids. I read that too. It works by decomposing the tissue around the bite into a runny sort of slurry the spider can drink up at their leisure.

I saw one last week in a webby little corner just slurping down on a cave cricket three times its own size. That cricket had kept me up sawing away at its back legs for like two nights in my closet.

So who's sleeping tonight! I am, that's who. And that's all I have to say about that noisy old cricket.

I do—I'll be honest—I do wish I could see my niece again. She's so fun and creative. She brightens up this big old barn. I know you folks at the Historical Society call it a "mansion," which is a bit much.

It's taken care of so many of us. Both of my grandfathers built it together when they moved to town and three generations of us have come up here. But not four. I guess I think that's a shame.

I swear it's not hard to be mindful of the spiders and as long as...What's that? Oh, you mean this?

It's not a cast, it's a sling. I've lost some mobility to a new bite on my shoulder. Bored a little hole right through the deltoid, the doctor said. And now, temporarily I promise you, I have to wear this.

Of course not, it's fine, I just—Well now don't be ridiculous. No one's more careful than me.

Mœrlin's Keep

I take the wizard for a circus clown
leaping thrashing about the street in purple
among traveling carnival folk uproarious
spitting yellow fireballs across the tip of his staff
flinging coins at children grabbing giggling

Silver bits gleam in the mudded street
filth and pebbles grime houses and shops
sun draws up hot stinking mists only
fair Camelot rises immune, pale
pendulous thunderheads afar

Hair and beard whip about livid-stone
face, eyes burn white smith's fire
muscles strain dark lines against their mates
a jet of steam from a nostril: curious way to laugh
a face before mine, a voice behind my ear
I question nothing

Now what I must describe as music
grave, powerful, tragic to drown felicity
celebrate, praise, weep to drown felicity
candle flicker and spike of ice
felled from a winter eve into an upraised eye
when gone I dread and wish its return

Song of the Lost

A humming creature lives in the woods
Or behind the nearest dune in the dessert
Under the ocean—anywhere you're lost

She hums the song you sang as a child
To keep yourself company in the dark sweating
In the bathroom at your cousin's birthday

Before the others formed a big grinning circle
For a game to which everyone else already knew
The rules and, seemingly, who would win

Maybe it's a hymn, maybe a bubblegum bop
Or, I don't know, the national anthem of Canada
She knows them all, every one you might've sung

Her version promises a path, but not comfort
Perhaps a squeaking aluminum ladder propped
Across a land-slid gully, lively with eels

The creature lies that she can lead you home
You follow despite the lie, or because of it
Her music feels as good a shelter as any, when lost

The One Who Walks

Alexis White set out to walk the dog
Soon caught his breath upon a shaded log
Paused to switch his music track and stretch
Unzipped his pack, forgot to close the catch

The log was damp and much had gone to seed
Poor Goose, the pup, quivered on her lead
Cool morning mist lay thick upon the ground
Alas! Alexis stood, did not turn round

A rustle, slither, coiled up from the deeps
It whispers in his mind now as he sleeps
What had crept from log to pack unseen?
By day it walks the dog, the man between

Sawgrass

See now an old thoroughfare trod
By generations of hooves, claws, and paws
It once cut a comfortable scar, remarkably
Straight, across the shallows of Moon Bog
From Black Grove to the foot of Star Mount

Sawgrass rises eight and nine feet high
In swaying spires that could chunk as deeply
Into a man's arm as a swung machete
Hanks of coarse brown and white fur cling to
Toothed edges, snagged souvenirs of passers-by

Bog birch roots green veins of brown and white
Claw upward thorugh the muck miming
Fingers of the dead through grave dirt
A mere trick of the light—no dead here
For immeasureable years, only a place of transit

Yet we witness a near miss with a fawn, startled
By the sharp crack of gunfire—for the fawn
A starter's pistol to a race into a thatch of knives
He bucks in panic, as any of us might, spotted
Fur flexing, twisting, sharp red on sharper green

And then she comes, with her song, quiet
Penetrating; the fawn slows, shivers, weeps
Thick blood from a hundred small slices
Another pistol crack rolls acrid in the woods
The witch cocks an ear, no more than that

She sings, hums, draws back the sawgrass blade
By blade, clasped between forefinger and thumb
The mother doe snorts, forelegs splayed ready
To charge, slash, kick, bite the visitor then
She picks up the song, a soft bray to calm

Work done at last the witch makes space
Fawn rises, mother doe honks courage
Witch retreats, not invited to the reunion
Fawn sways with the doe's licks, first of many
And shivers again—licks and shivers to heal

The lasting harm of a moment

Bound

She died young
They bound her jaw
With a clean tea towel

Her daughters lived
Long hanging tea towels
From every rod in the house

Unspent grief fluttering
Bleached linen shrouds
With every step

His Terrible Nephew

When the Liar imported his terrible nephew to town, the Whitton whisper network unearthed a calcified word like archaeologists dry-brushing a Tyrannosaurus thigh bone from a badlands hillside. That single word was "trouble."

Speculation on the exact manner of trouble reflected back onto each whispering archaeologist without any basis or excavation of fact. Mathilda Givens, for example, an eleventh grader with her own terrible kin, gushed that the boy had arrived in Whitton exuding "woman trouble."

Harmon Tryce, a former postal worker who retired precicely one day after delivering a stack of skin mags to the home mailbox—not the secret P.O. Box—of Pastor Skaggs, grunted that the terrible nephew suffered from "legal trouble."

Pastor Skaggs himself—he of the other P.O. Box that the new postman would surely visit more faithfully than his predecessor—declaimed from the pulpit in dry-brush-soft murmurs that the boy experienced "spiritual trouble," and needed to GET RIGHT WITH THE LORD™.

That two of the town's rumor archaeologists had brushed and sifted partial truths mattered not in the end, as no Whitton law required the boy to register what he had done. (Oddly, no one guessed "money trouble," likely owing to the bile-inducing wealth of the Liar himself who, remember, was the boy's uncle.)

We keep calling this boy "boy," which certainly all 19-year-old boys are, unless enough of us wish them jailed or executed, and at first no one did. He was good looking if he closed his eyes. His brown hair fluffed over in a blow-dried swoop, and his clothes fit him very well.

His uncle gave him a gun: a .357 Magnum, smooth machined silver with a custom grip of glossy tan material that resembled tiger's eye gemstones. Why? Well, deer were eating the Liar's manicured garden flowers off the back patio.

They appeared mornings, stepping sedately through the rioting bamboo grove to chew heads off drooping daylilies and dahlias. The Liar watched seething from his kitchen window as a doe and her spotted fawn stripped vibrant red petals from an amur honeysuckle bush as if sharing licks off a cone of raspberry sherbet.

And so he set his terrible nephew to watch with his silver .357 Magnum with the faux tiger's eye grip.

Tensions flared on the first day when the boy took aim at a puffy little wren perched on the lip of one of the hanging feeders. He had never fired gun before, but the wren evaporated in a white cloud of dust and feathers that looked like hand grenade had gone off inside a roll of quilted toilet paper.

The Liar didn't like songbirds, exactly—he didn't like anything at all, as we established earlier—but he knew that *other* people like songbirds, and some even keep track of birdsong on a phone app that the Liar downloaded the moment he learned of it. *Collecting* he understood, and he set out at once to create the largest collection of bird calls around. (Crucially, he also learned how to compare his collection with others in the region.)

He made it clear to his terrible nephew that birds were to be spared from the garden purge. It was deer, and only deer, on whom he sought revenge for decimating his flower garden.

And revenge he got, through his terrible nephew. It was as bad as you're imagining; likely worse. When the deer did not arrive immediately—scenting, perhaps, danger in new, slippery fragrances of gun oil and male rage—the Liar purchased sacks of deer feed to scatter among the ragged, decaying flower stems.

He spread the feed, the deer came, and the boy shot them. Not well. The swift death of the wren had been beginner's luck after all. They attempted to sell the venison in town, but no one bought it.

So he made his terrible nephew drag the carcasses into the woods just beyond the property line where they rotted, raising a terrible stink that for weeks permeated the back garden, mixing with the sweet, heavy odor of amur honeysuckle, which, in the absence of deer, rapidly overran and throttled all of the other flowers in the garden.

de Vampier

I am descended of vampyres
who long ago shunned bite and suck
who spat curled fangs into the dust as milkteeth

Imagine the barbarity of driving dog-named
spurs of exposed bone into a neighbor's pulse
rubbing tongue over wet ragged wobble-edges

When the soul, that torrential spark
we pretend we cannot see, feeds
generations deathlessly starving

I drank of my ancestors and they of me

I dined fangless piercing with frontier-grown
tendrils of the mind, shoots keen and hollow, an
infinite octopus of undulating hypodermic lust

Then, a realization, a mirror, the hiss of aeons
Drinking souls just perpetuates hunger, mine
and yours, I tell the coin-eyed army at my back

More hisses into becaped elbows—shame
tantrums of the dead. Yet. Among the sibilance
new sparks, dusty soul engines flaring

Timidly daring to heal

Ring Around the Rosie

One greater dead puppets many lesser
Who tangle to the living like marionettes flung
Against the gleaming shaft of a May Pole

Enough tethers and even the living cannot help
but notice—they slow and frown, sigh,
"Must've slept weird last night."

While that one slavering ghoul dredges itself
Upward on spiral arms of an ancestral galaxy
Devouring existence, defecating exhaustion

What Follows

What must it look like, this terrible pursuer?
Its sound like potatoes in burlap—tossed, dragged
A metronome that thumps and slithers
One lurch nearer, always nearer, always toward

There it comes again—you must hear it too—
Grating across the ceiling tile in the upstairs hall?
Shoving a lidless eye through liminal cobwebs
The soft drift of spider lace across a gray cheek

Another thump, another almost plaintive rasp
I feel for it in long stretches of dark and night
Pursuit cannot have been meant to last forever
Still I am the one to veer away, reset the distance

And then one day, my daughter: "What is that?"
Peering backward through an empty doorway
"What is that?" asks my son, frowning at the ceiling
The cat lays back its ears and spits at nothing

I draw a butter knife from the kitchen drawer
Faded wallpaper with sunflowers the color of bone
Lines the drawer bottom, taut and brittle
As the desiccated scalp of a mummy in museum

The butter knife saws through the ceiling drywall
Fine white dust sifts down like confectioner's sugar
Frantic scrabbling thuds from somewhere above
My children stumble back and clutch at each other

I pull away handfuls of drywall in messy clots
Crumbled gypsum and long ragged paper
A halo of dust circumscribes the chair I stand on
Soils the carpet I laid when my daughter was born

I step up onto the hard, curved chair back
The children gasp; "Don't worry a bit," I say
Confidently, I thrust my head and shoulders up
Through the untidy hole I tore into my own house

The dry, stale musk of time sears my nose
When the gloom dithers I see a shape: this thing
That has skulked along at my heels since ever
A chronic earthquake built into my foundation

At first it defies seeing, abhors detail—except
A round, tormented eye planted in shadow
Like an acorn plugged in rancid mud, edges moldy
Filthy masses—hair?—frame the eye, explode out

"Let's have no more," I say. "Enough is enough."
The central eye widens further, glistening
In the stark new light from the hole I carved
"We're all done with this." I reach out. "No more."

The shape quakes, rattles the rafters, emits
A cloud of grime like ink from a cornered cuttlefish
"What!" shouts my son. "Dad!" calls my daughter.
"It's fine," I assure those whose peril drove me here

Though it isn't precisely fine, nor is it a lie
This moment between my pursuer and me
The inevitability of being caught, long in coming
And only one of us can imagine what to do next

The Witch

Head bowed to the night
A harsh orange rime of flame
Cupped in rough fingers

Eva

Eva, wronged, called for dragons
The others groaned and rolled their eyes
But no dragon, they reasoned, would
Listen to the girl, and so, all burned
Firestorms whipped under leather wings
Roaring Eva astride the golden neck while
They, aghast, called her wicked

Mudslide

The builders mined for tree roots, pulled up
every tendril, vein, and nerve, capillaries of soil
collapsing around cultivated vacuum

They could have told the owner what
it meant, these millions of tubular cave-ins
this extraction of ground memory

As he rose and fell on the balls of his tiny feet
surfing a wave of hang-ten ego watching
a cement truck pour a cement root canal

Mammatus clouds one evening in late spring
dusk ripe peaches bobbing over the land
long, low rumbles from the southeast

The Liar splayed in his garden hosting no one
when the first pendulous rain drop splatted
across the rim of his glasses like a rotten grape

He sputtered cursed vowed to build a roof
over his garden of sun hungry ornamentals
and staggered up to his new mansion

Forearms crooked protectively overhead while
fat payloads of rain hammered and bored
into sore, bruised clumps of earth

The hilltop was old even as hilltops go, had
weathered ten thousand million rainstorms since
thrusting up amid the crash of continental plates

In that time nothing like this terrible man or his
terrible house had been visited upon the hill;
no harm so fundamental in half a billion years

Of the storm, a guard down at the motorized gate
said it looked like a rain cloaked kaiju from a
sci-fi picture tackled the house from behind

It lurched and leapt between flashes of lightning
as the soil around the foundation succumbed
coaxing the house into a terminal downhill jam

To crash splinter shatter against the painted steel
fence around the base of the hill, townsfolk
staring out their windows, feeling all they felt

As a lightning nickelodeon flashed
the stopmotion ruin of house and man
down the slopes of Star Mount

The town's oldest and most beloved landmark
They wondered petrified who among them
had wished hard enough for it to come true

Before You Go

Before you go, leave no
Chip, chunk, or gobbet
To fester and haunt

Not the amorphous tumor
Sloughed off in the sofa cushions
Crunchy with teeth, fibrous with hair

Not the speck lodged like sharp silica
In the mucosal duct of your sister's eye socket
To redden and weep in the nighttime mirror

Not the shard of shrapnel shot
Into the trembling thimble of your
Baby's heart well before he was born

Before you go, if not before that,
Push, scream, kick, strain, *fight,* goddammit
To defy the press of ages and become whole

PLAYS

UNQUIET

A Play in 10 Minutes

by André Swartley

Cast of Characters

Maximillian Chambers:	A boy of 14.
Heather Chambers:	A woman in her early 40s; Max's mother.
Albert Chambers:	A man in his early 40s; Max's father.
Shadow 1:	A masked figure in all black.
Shadow 2:	A masked figure in all black.

Scene

A family home in the USA.

Time

The present.

Scene 1

SETTING: We are in the living room of the Chambers, a middle-class family of three in the Midwestern US. A long sofa is at center. If our surroundings were visible, we might see a bookcase filled with cookbooks and pop fiction. We might see a smattering of junk mail and pocket change cast across the table of the adjoining dining room. But instead we see the sofa, surrounded by blackness.

AT RISE: MAXIMILLIAN CHAMBERS squats on the sofa, feet tucked under his bottom, staring straight ahead. A bright light, tightly focused, shines in his eyes. An ambient, grinding, industrial sound fills the room. At downstage right, two masked figures all in black seem to be discussing something. Their gestures are 'normal,' but their speech is distorted, inhuman. After several seconds, MAX pulls a pair of tinted glasses from his pocket. From the other pocket comes a pair of ear buds, which he pops into his ears. The room goes completely dark. Lights come up slowly. MAX is still where he was, but the two SHADOWS have now resolved into his parents, HEATHER and ALBERT CHAMBERS. The industrial sound and spotlight are gone. ALBERT is reading a letter while HEATHER stands by.

ALBERT
(Finishing the letter)
Okay, so when should schedule the meeting?

HEATHER
Don't say it like that.

ALBERT
How am I supposed to say it? Half my vacation last year evaporated to

meetings with school teachers. If it keeps up this year, I'm going to have to start taking unpaid time off.

            HEATHER
You don't have to go.

            ALBERT
Sure, and leave you to sit alone on one side of a conference room table, getting grilled like some crook hauled in by the police?

            HEATHER
That's a bit much.

            ALBERT
It's how I feel, going in there, having to nod and smile while they tell me I'm a bad father.

            HEATHER
No one has ever said that. And if they did criticize our parenting, it would be mine. It's always the mom's fault. Too lenient, too strict, not involved enough, helicopter mom,

breast fed too long. Go online if you don't believe me. There are about ten billion articles and chat rooms where moms can find out all the ways they're wrecking their kids.

ALBERT

That's idiotic. You shouldn't ever have to feel that way.

HEATHER

I don't. I'm just saying, if you want an easy target, the mom always has a giant one painted across her forehead. Not the dad. Last time we went in, the counselor thanked you about five times just for coming. Not that I don't appreciate it. I'm glad you want to be involved.

ALBERT

Yeah, hooray for me. But what happens this time? Or the next? Will they keep thanking us over and over again for the next four years? Bet I'll get a huge thanks when I have to quit my job to go to these meetings.

HEATHER

Now you're blaming him.

ALBERT

There's a pretty short list of suspects.

HEATHER

You keep talking about this like it's a crime. The only specific concern the letter mentioned was the ear buds, and even that sounded pretty tame. They just want to talk.

ALBERT

Right. It's always just talk. Talking and thanking. At the junior high, and before that. Every time we walk into a principal's office they say, 'Thanks for coming again. Here's your coffee, Heather, two creams and no sugar, just the way you like it. Albert, here's one of those rootbeer candies you like so goddamn much.' The only difference I've seen is whether they think Max *is* on drugs or *should be* on drugs.

                    HEATHER
Come on, we've walked out of every one of those meetings with a plan.

                    ALBERT
Yeah, for one class, and then it's on to the next. We could paper the walls with plans by this point. The Speech Pathologist's was my favorite because she only used green paper. What I want to know is, when do we get the plan where we don't have to talk about plans anymore?

                    HEATHER
You're frustrated. It's okay. Maybe go upstairs and cool off for a bit. I can talk to Max.

                    ALBERT
And say what? Are you going to congratulate him for introducing us to his newest principal? That's three for three, son. A disciplinary hat trick!

HEATHER
This is not his fault.

ALBERT
Whose then? All you've ever done is make excuses for him. Did you ever think maybe you painted that big old target on your own forehead?

> (Shocked silence. Until now the argument has felt familiar. On the sofa, MAX fidgets, scratches at seams of his jeans.)

ALBERT
Aw, crap. I'm sorry.

HEATHER
I see.

ALBERT
Really. That wasn't okay. I'm sorry.

HEATHER
I know what you think of me as a mom. Maybe it's time you said it out loud.

(A power seems to be growing around HEATHER. She is steeling herself for something.)

ALBERT
Wait, please. That came out wrong.

HEATHER
Okay, I'll wait.

ALBERT
It's just...

(beat)

He's never had to take any responsibility. I wish you could see that.

HEATHER
I wish you could see how hard he works.

ALBERT
I wish you could see what he does to you. I wouldn't call it manipulation, exactly, but--

HEATHER

And I wish I didn't have to stand between you and him.

ALBERT

You stand between him and everything. Why should I be any different?

   (Sags, exhausted, disgusted with self.)

That's terrible. I'm being terrible. I just thought that by the time he went to high school all this would be sorted out. I thought he'd be able to function. I thought we would finally get to go on trips. Do some of the things we talked about when we were dating. We weren't much older than he is.

HEATHER
   (softening)
It just isn't the time...

ALBERT
It never is.

(ALBERT takes a deep breath, turns to MAX)

ALBERT (cont'd)
Well, Max, can you fill us in? Your teacher Mr. Kennedy wants us to come in for a chat.

(The intense spotlight from before begins to shine into Max's eyes again.)

MAX
I don't know.

ALBERT
That's not going to fly anymore, bucko. You're in high school now. Nearly a man grown, as they say.

HEATHER
Mr. Kennedy says he's asked you to take out your ear buds in class.

MAX
I can hear him fine.

ALBERT

I guess he'd rather have your full attention.

    (MAX doesn't answer.)

I guess I would, too.

    (ALBERT strides over and yanks the earbuds out of MAX's ears. The stage lights flicker. The grinding industrial hum from earlier kicks up again.)

HEATHER

Albert!

ALBERT

I bought these for you, with money from the job I keep having to miss because you get in trouble at school.

    (HEATHER retrieves the ear buds from ALBERT and returns them to MAX, who does not put them on.)

HEATHER

Go upstairs, Albert. Or better yet, go take a drive. Get a soda and come back when you're calmer.

> (The industrial noise increases in volume. A black gloved hand appears over the back of the sofa and SHADOW 1 emerges to perch on the back of the sofa behind MAX. SHADOW 2 slinks out from under the sofa and crouches at MAX's feet. Both begin to poke him gently on different parts of his body.)

ALBERT

There you go, Heather, standing between him and responsibility again.

HEATHER

I'm standing between him and you.

ALBERT

It's been a decade of this. I just want it to stop!

HEATHER

Do you think he can control any of this? Look at him!

> (SHADOW 1 and SHADOW 2 are poking MAX more insistently now. MAX twitches with each poke.)

HEATHER

Do you think you can yell it out of him or make him run laps like a football coach?

ALBERT

School wasn't easy for me, either. But I buckled down and my parents didn't get called in to talk to the principal every week. No one stood between me and the big bad world.

HEATHER

This isn't about you.

ALBERT

That's the truest thing you've said all night.

> (HEATHER turns away from ALBERT and hunkers in front of MAX, who is now rocking forward and back with the poking.)

ALBERT
Fourteen years of parenting together, and all it's done is drive us further and further apart.

> (HEATHER spins upward to face him again, crackling with the power we saw before.)

HEATHER
Did you just say that in front of our son?

ALBERT
He can't hear anything when he's like this. I'm just finally speaking the tru--

HEATHER
Out. Now. Come back if and when you can apologize and actually mean it.

ALBERT
Are you really asking me to leave? Is that where this is going? After all this time?

    (HEATHER does not respond. She has drawn her line in the sand. ALBERT steps toward MAX.)

HEATHER
What are you doing?

ALBERT
Max, I want you to look your old man in the eye.

    (ALBERT reaches out to take off MAX'S sunglasses. SHADOW 1 and SHADOW 2 start into a frenzy of poking and scratching all over MAX'S body and face. MAX lashes out and kicks ALBERT hard enough to knock him over. The SHADOWS retreat to both ends of the sofa and crouch like gargoyles. ALBERT scrambles up. HEATHER instinctively dives between them.)

                    ALBERT
What are you protecting him for? I wasn't going to hurt him.

                    HEATHER
Please just go.

   (After a beat, ALBERT walks slowly off-stage. HEATHER moves like she is going to call him back, but stops. A door slams. Heather looks on, hand pressed to her mouth. SHADOWS 1 and 2 are creeping back toward MAX. HEATHER collects herself and turns to MAX. She reaches out to touch MAX'S head, but catches herself. Instead she lowers herself onto the arm of the sofa and watches MAX. Stage lights begin to dim until the only the bright spotlight remains on MAX'S face. He finally replaces his ear buds as the industrial grinding sound grows louder and louder and the SHADOWS tentatively begin to poke at him once more.)
(FADE OUT)

(END OF SCENE)

HOW THE OCTOPUS GOT HIS LEGS

A Play in 10 Minutes
by André Swartley

Cast of Characters

Narrator: A woman's voice.
Spider: A woman in costume voiced by a piccolo.
Octopus: A man in costume plus other performers in black voiced by a cello.
Life: Figures in costume.

Scene
The shores of the early universe.
Time
Billions of years ago.

Scene 1

SETTING: A dark cosmic beach strewn with sea creatures and debris

AT RISE: The NARRATOR's dialogue begins rise. At the appropriate time, the curtain rises to reveal the SPIDER, OCTOPUS, and other LIFE laying onstage with the rest of the debris.

NARRATOR
One moment, long ago, a spark ignited in the winds and gnashing teeth of Chaos. The spark was the mind of a Creator, so fiercely imaginative and rebellious that she brought herself into being. And from her, the universe exploded.

   (Light, sound)

NARRATOR
The Chaos fought back against the intruder the way a wave crashes against a sparkling shore. But the Creator snatched at the winds of Chaos and twisted them into bizarre forms to populate her newborn universe.

> (Curtain rises; things like sea creatures litter the stage, some props, some actors)

NARRATOR
When the dark tide receded, these new hiccups of the Creator's mind remained, gasping, floundering on the virgin sands of space and time. Life, the marriage of Chaos and Creation, had begun. And it was afraid.

> (More light and sound; brightly-colored shapes struggle in their bodies)

NARRATOR
The Creator did not—could not—keep still. Among the accidental life rose

a new, deliberate one. A Spider, quick, light, intelligent.

> (One of the shapes on stage stands and surveys herself; a piccolo tweets)

NARRATOR
The Spider saw anxiety and confusion in the lives around her and experienced something the blind, boiling creativity of the Creator could never manage on its own: care. The Spider on her many legs dashed around, helping others who were stranded and frightened in the new world by crafting soft beds and protective cocoons with her webbing.

> (SPIDER lays a hammock across a quivering shape and it stills)

NARRATOR
Some felt safety in the Spider's web, but others continued to despair. Their new bodies screamed with sensation, with dark and light, with heat

and cold. Where the Spider's web did not calm, her venom granted the rest they craved. And when their souls returned to the mind of the Creator, their bodies nourished the Spider so she could continue on. Soon the creatures begin to love the Spider. It was at this time that the first word rose from the sands of the universe, and the creatures bestowed it upon the Spider: Mother.

    (All lights down)

NARRATOR

Nimble though she was, the mother Spider was not fast enough to help everyone. Some life perished in desperation, still gasping and alone. Conversely, unknown to the Spider, a new type of creature was rising to prominence.

    (Lights up; something like a bean bag stretches upward as the shape inside it stands)

NARRATOR

This new life could not move, for its body was only a soft, shapeless bag. But that bag was wrapped around the universe's most powerful brain. It felt the light skitter of the Spider as she made her rounds, and it wanted to see her. So it grew eyes.

(The shape turns around to reveal eyes on the back of the costume)

NARRATOR

This new, clever brain bag watched the Spider work.

(More piccolo tweeting)

NARRATOR

And suddenly the brain bag was moved.

(A groaning sound; a gloved hand on cello strings)

NARRATOR

Once again, it willed its body to grow and change.

(A figure in black unrolls a length of cloth out from the central body of the beanbag shape)

                    NARRATOR
Though the brain bag was not fast like the Spider, it had a long reach, and it could sweep frightened beings toward the Spider for whatever comforts they desired.

(The figure in black uses the long strip of cloth to draw one of the creatures toward the SPIDER)

                    NARRATOR
And so the brain bag and the Spider created a third new concept in this struggling universe: cooperation.

(All lights down)

                    NARRATOR
With no other alternatives available, time continued to pass.

> (Lights up; the "life" on stage appears more orderly than before; additional strips of cloth now extend from the beanbag shape, with black-clad figures making them undulate)

NARRATOR
The brain bag continued to grow legs until he had nine—one more than the Spider. He invented a fancy name for himself too: Enneapus. He took on more and more of the responsibilities of caring for the other lives on the shore, believing he did it better than she.

> (Black figures continue arranging "life" in rigidly ordered rows and block the SPIDER from accessing them)

NARRATOR
But his version of care brought no comfort to anyone except himself. The Spider could hear cries of "Mother! Mother!" but could not reach them

due to the Enneapus's interference.
At last, frustrated to the point of
violence, the Spider bit one of the
Enneapus's tentacles, causing it to
wither.

> (Sharp tweet from piccolo; ag-
> grieved groan from cello; one
> figure in black drops its strip
> of cloth, which drifts to the
> ground)

NARRATOR

The Enneapus's remaining tentacles
flailed in distress, scattering the
previously ordered life across the
shore. But the Spider did not tend to
them. She used her powerful webbing
to suspend the Enneapus's poisoned
tentacle in the air.

> (Stage hands bring a ladder to
> the stage; the SPIDER carries one
> end of the cloth up to the top
> of the ladder so that it makes a
> vertical line in the air)

NARRATOR

Thus the Spider made yet another creation from the dead and frozen limb: a tree. There she roosted, high over the shore so that she could no longer hear the cries of those below. And from her sadness came two more inventions: the rain and the ocean. Some creatures learned they could swim. Others drowned where they lay.

(Blue light plays across the bottom half of the stage)

NARRATOR

So the Enneapus, who could have helped to create love, instead created remorse. He skulked at the bottom of the Spider's ocean of tears, ashamed. He took on a new name to reflect the loss of a tentacle: Octopus. Yet he never attempted to separate the dead limb, choosing, at his own peril, to keep all nine connected to his body as a grim monument to the cost of cleverness without caring.

(Lights fade but do not go down completely)

NARRATOR

The Spider remained in the tree for the rest of her life, although her young did not. She taught them how to care for each other, then to spin their webs into lacy wings that could ride the wind to all corners of the young universe to carry on her work.

(Delighted piccolo chirping)

NARRATOR

As for the Octopus, the Spider's venom eventually traveled from his bitten tentacle to his mighty brain, and he died before his time. Like the spider, he had multiplied. More and more octopuses sprang up in the depths of the ocean, but to this day they live short lives, full of creativity, cleverness, and isolation. Penance for throwing away the universe's first love.

(FADE OUT)

(END OF SCENE)

THE GIRL WHO COULD FLY

A Play in 10 Minutes

by André Swartley

Cast of Characters

Sam: A university student.
Gem: A university student.
Mel: A university student.
Bobby: A university student.
Director: A university official.

Scene

A large university in the US.

Time

The present.

Scene 1

SETTING: A women's dorm room set up at Stage Right. A cot and sofa sit parallel with a computer desk behind.
AT RISE: SAM sits on the edge of the cot, facing her friends MEL and GEM.

SAM
So, yeah. I guess that's it. Huh. Didn't take as long to explain as I thought.

MEL
I don't get it.

   (Beat)

SAM
Which...What? What don't you get? It's pretty straightforward.

GEM
Do you have to, like, flap your arms or something?

SAM

Nope. Just straight up in the air. Pow.

MEL

I don't believe it.

GEM

No, this makes total sense.

SAM

(Laughing)
It does?

GEM

But why are you telling us now? Why not before?

MEL

Or never.

SAM

My mom said I should be more open with people. Like, people who are good at singing or soccer or whatever don't have to hide what they can do. They go out and perform.

                    GEM
You want to perform? For who?

                    MEL
The circus.

                    SAM
No, I'm just...are you mad? Mel?

    (Lights down)

    (Lights up—a crowded hallway.
    SAM and GEM are walking together.
    BOBBY runs to catch up to them.)

                    BOBBY
Hey! Yo! Hey, fly girl! Wait up! Stop!

                    SAM
Um, get your hand off me. Do I know you?

                    BOBBY
You're that girl who can fly, right?

                    SAM
Excuse me?

GEM

Who told you that?

BOBBY

Is it true?

SAM

Yes.

BOBBY

Awesome. I've got something kind of weird to ask you.

SAM

The answer is definitely no.

    (She turns to go. BOBBY grabs her again.)

Oh my God, my body is not your body. If you're trying to make me fly away so I don't have to deal with you anymore, just keep up whatever this is.

BOBBY

Be cool a second. This is important. My name is Bobby Mann.

GEM

Mann? As in Mann Hall?

BOBBY

My grandpa.

SAM

And Mann Stadium?

BOBBY

My uncles.

SAM

Well, I don't know who told you about the flying thing, and as cool as it is to meet the slab of uncooked white meat behind the trust fund, I don't take other people on rides for pleasure or riches. I'm not one of your uncle's Cessnas.

BOBBY

Will you just stop? Okay, I know you can fly, and you know my family is rich. We're even. Please just listen.

GEM

He seems really worried.

SAM

Fine.

(BOBBY glances around as if to check for eavesdroppers.)

BOBBY

Okay. I'm pledging Beta Theta Psi.

SAM

Gross.

BOBBY

It's a family thing. Anyway, there's one part of the process that pledges almost never do.

SAM

Lemme guess. You have to touch butts in the shower but make it look like an accident?

GEM

Sam, come on.

BOBBY
There's a secret group in the fraternity. It's like, more elite than—

GEM and SAM
Crossbones?

BOBBY
How do you know that?

(SAM twirls a finger as if to say, *Keep it moving.*)

BOBBY
Okay, you're so smart, do you know what a pledge has to do to get into Crossbones in his first year? Well, this is where you come in. The pledge has to push a girl out of a window.

SAM
What the fuck?

BOBBY
Or over a balcony, or off a roof. She has to fall at least fifteen feet in order to—Hey! Where are you going?

(BOBBY grabs Sam's arm again. SAM jerks out of his grasp.)

SAM
Dude, seriously, if you touch me again I will throw YOU out the nearest window.

BOBBY
No, you don't get it. You're not supposed to hurt the girl. There's supposed to be a mattress or a trampoline or a group of guys with parachute underneath or something.

(GEM bursts out laughing.)

GEM
Mel put you up to this, didn't she?

BOBBY
Yeah. She was the one who told me Sam could fly. You know her, right?

SAM
She was our friend. Emphasis on the was.

GEM

I did not know she had it in her. Bravo.

BOBBY

So you'll do it?

SAM

Do what?

BOBBY

Well, if you can really fly, then I don't have to worry about the mattress or anything.

GEM

Okay, ha ha. You got us. Prank's over, moneybags. Go back to your mansion and high five all your butlers.

(Beat.)

SAM

It's not a prank, is it? Mel told you I could fly and you came up with this idea.

(BOBBY digs in pockets and pulls out an old, browning piece of paper with a handwritten note.)

BOBBY
I know I shouldn't show you this, but here's the instructions from the Crossbones Founders. I have to do it before sundown tonight. That's why I came to you as soon as I heard. I don't want to hurt anyone.

SAM
This says the girl can't know what's happening. So by telling me about this, you're violating the rules.

BOBBY
I...I don't want to hurt anyone.

SAM
Never, ever speak to me again. About anything. Do you understand?

(Lights down)

(Lights up—An administrator's office at Stage Left. DIRECTOR sits behind a desk opposite SAM.)

DIRECTOR

Sam, thank you for coming. Do you know why I called you in here?

SAM

No. I'm sorry, I'm not actually sure who you are.

DIRECTOR

Understandable. You haven't had any reason to come into contact with us in your time here. My name is Leland Woodward. I'm the Director of the Office of Student Conduct.

SAM

You deal with students who get into trouble.

DIRECTOR

Succinctly put. Yes. That is what we do. Now do you know why I called you in here?

                    SAM
Okay, yes. Thank you for address-
ing my complaint so quickly. I wasn't
sure anyone would believe me.

                　DIRECTOR
Believe you? That you can fly?

                    SAM
No. What? I turned in a complaint
yesterday that this guy, Bobby Mann,
asked me if he could shove me out of
a window as part of a frat pledge. Oh
my God. Did he push someone out of a
window?

                　DIRECTOR
This is a very serious situation,
Sam. Mr. Mann approached you because
he heard a rumor that you can fly. Is
that correct?

                    SAM
That's what he told me.

                　DIRECTOR
Can you?

SAM

Yes, I can. But that doesn't stop me getting sliced up by broken glass, does it? Did you already know about this? The window pushing thing?

DIRECTOR

Mr. Mann also showed you a document.

SAM

If you can call it that. It looked like it was written by a two year old on a torn grocery bag.

DIRECTOR

The document clearly stated that it didn't have to be a window.

SAM

What?

DIRECTOR

It could be a staircase or a balcony or, as was the case last night, the roof of a building.

(SAM leaps to her feet.)

SAM

What? What do you mean? Did he push someone? Who—Is she okay?

DIRECTOR

She is not okay, Sam. Not the way you would have been, if he had pushed you.

SAM

I'm not sure what you're saying.

DIRECTOR

Would you be able to carry a person while you are flying?

SAM

What?

DIRECTOR

You seem like a strong young woman. Could you hold someone in your arms while you fly? Someone small, of course. Not a football player or anything like that.

SAM
Please tell me whoever Bobby Mann pushed is still alive.

DIRECTOR
Allegedly pushed, Sam. We do not have all of the evidence yet.

SAM
You just told me you know about Bobby's "document" that talks about pushing girls out of windows!

DIRECTOR
Your friend Mel is several inches shorter and lighter than you, correct?

SAM
Wait, did he push Mel? Where is she?

DIRECTOR
She is in the hospital. She says you could have saved her.

SAM
You think this is my fault?

DIRECTOR

If you can fly, you would have been unharmed from the fall. Or you could have caught your friend and lowered her to the ground safely. But you did neither of those things. Why?

SAM

What is happening here? Look, I didn't know he was going to push her off a building!

DIRECTOR

You reported that he was going to do so yesterday afternoon, several hours before the actual event. You were in the best position to save your friend, were you not?

SAM

Okay, I feel like we're done here. I'm going to go check on my friend.

DIRECTOR

You may go, for now. But I am afraid Mel has asked that we instruct you not to visit her.

SAM

Whatever.

(DIRECTOR stands too.)

DIRECTOR

College is a time when people have to make hard choices, Sam. Grown-up choices. Unselfish choices. No one died this time, thank God. But it could have gone much differently.

> (SAM runs out of the office to center stage, throws her backpack to the side and poses like she is going to take off. After a moment, she picks up the pack and heaves it over her shoulder. She turns slowly to EXIT Stage Right.)

(FADE OUT)

(END OF SCENE)

Regarding Performances

Just like poems are meant to be heard as well as read on the page, plays are meant to be performed for an audience. I wrote the preceding three ten-minute plays for the Pen to Paper to Performance program at Hesston College in 2017, 2018, and 2019. They were directed by Rachel Jantzi and performed by Hesston College students, faculty, and community members.

Anyone wishing to produce these plays publicly in the future has my permission and my blessing. Break a leg!

André Swartley

Acknowledgments

Special thanks first and always to Kate for giving space and encouragement keep writing and also to try new things. Thanks to my kids for fresh perspectives on literally everything, and for motivating me to seek out whatever truths I was able to find in the writing of this book. I spend every day in awe of their creativity.

Thanks to Dr. Stephanie Krehbiel, who was my first reader for this volume, and whose generous feedback gave me the confidence to keep pressing forward with a project so deeply unlike anything I've done before.

Thanks, finally, to the spirits and the dragons. The good ones, I mean. They know who they are.

About the Author

André Swartley is the author of five books, three of which received award nods: *The Island of Misfit Toys* was a finalist for the Best Books of Indiana in 2006; *Americanus Rex* was a finalist in the general fiction category of the Next Generation Indie Book Awards in 2009; and *Leon Martin and the Fantasy Girl* won First in Category in the 2013 Dante Rosetti Awards for young adult literature.

André teaches high school and lives with his family in Kansas.

www.ingramcontent.com/pod-product-compliance
Lightning Source LLC
Chambersburg PA
CBHW041925090426
42743CB00020B/3449